U.S. Sites and Symbols

★★★★★★★★★★★★

Natural Landmarks

Lauren Diemer

WEIGL PUBLISHERS INC.

Published by Weigl Publishers Inc.
350 5th Avenue, Suite 3304, PMB 6G
New York, NY 10118-0069

Website: www.weigl.com

Library of Congress Cataloging-in-Publication Data

Lauren Diemer.
 Natural landmarks / Lauren Diemer.
    p. cm. -- (U.S. sites and symbols)
 Includes index.
 ISBN 978-1-60596-146-0 (hard cover : alk. paper) -- ISBN 978-1-60596-147-7 (soft cover : alk. paper)
 1. Natural monuments--United States--Juvenile literature. 2. National Natural Landmarks Program (U.S.)--Juvenile literature. I. Title.
 QH76.H876 2010
 917.304'932--dc22
                                      2009005142

Printed in China
1 2 3 4 5 6 7 8 9 0 13 12 11 10 09

Editors: Deborah Lambert, Heather C. Hudak
Designer: Kathryn Livingstone

Photograph Credits

Contents

What are Symbols?

A symbol is an item that stands for something else. Objects, artworks, or living things can all be symbols. Every U.S. state has official symbols, or emblems. These items represent the people, history, and culture of the state. State symbols create feelings of pride and citizenship among the people who live there. Each of the 50 U.S. states has natural landmarks. These are a type of symbol.

National Landmarks History

The National Park Service in the United States recognizes important examples of nature in each state. National Natural Landmarks are those examples of nature that the National Park Service has recommended for conservation. These landmarks are places of **biological** and **geological** importance. There are fewer than 600 National Natural Landmarks in the United States.

Palo Duro Canyon State Park in Amarillo, Texas, became a National Natural Landmark in 1976. Collared lizards call this site home.

Finding Natural Landmarks by Region

Alaska

Hawai'i

Washington

Montana

Oregon

Idaho

Wyoming

The West

Nevada

Utah

Colorado

California

Arizona

New Mexico

Most states have natural landmarks. In this book, the states are ordered by region. These regions are the West, the Midwest, the South, and the Northeast. Each region is unique because of its land, people, and wildlife. Throughout this book, the regions are color coded. To find a natural landmark, first find the state using the map on this page. Then, turn to the pages that are the same color as that state.

North Dakota

Minnesota

South Dakota

Wisconsin

Michigan

The Midwest

Iowa

Nebraska

Indiana

Illinois

Ohio

West Virginia

Kansas

Missouri

Kentucky

Virginia

North Carolina

Oklahoma

Arkansas

Tennessee

The South

South Carolina

Georgia

Texas

Alabama

Mississippi

Louisiana

Florida

New Hampshire

Vermont

Maine

Massachusetts

The Northeast

New York

Rhode Island

Pennsylvania

Connecticut

New Jersey

Delaware

Maryland

Web Crawler

Find out facts about each state at **www.americaslibrary.gov**. Click on "Explore the States."

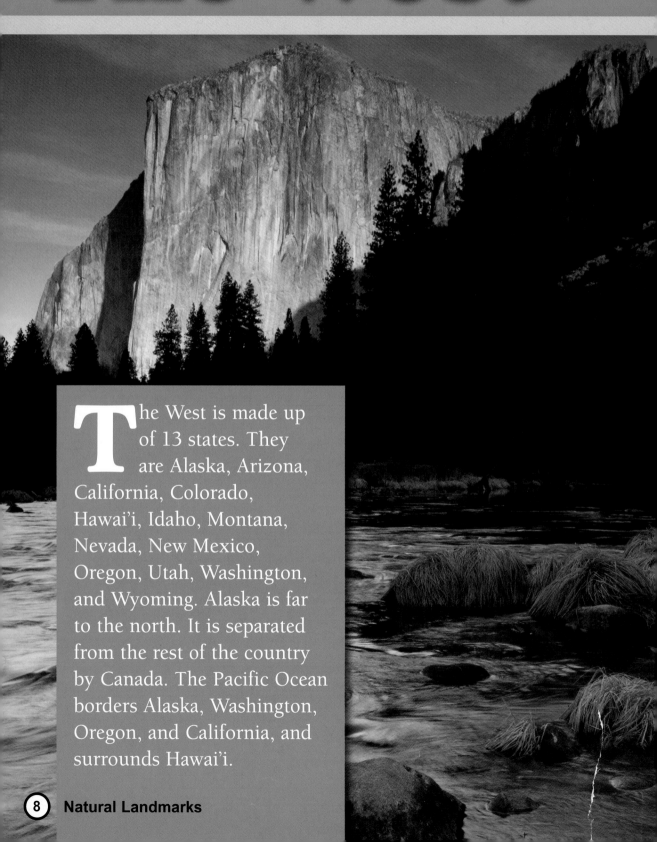

The West

The West is made up of 13 states. They are Alaska, Arizona, California, Colorado, Hawai'i, Idaho, Montana, Nevada, New Mexico, Oregon, Utah, Washington, and Wyoming. Alaska is far to the north. It is separated from the rest of the country by Canada. The Pacific Ocean borders Alaska, Washington, Oregon, and California, and surrounds Hawai'i.

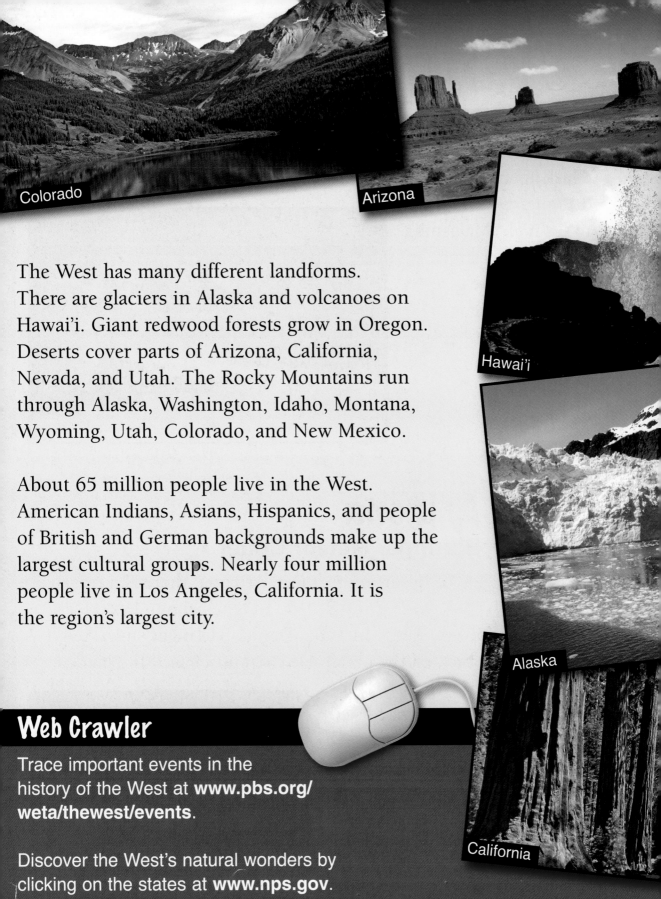

Colorado

Arizona

Hawai'i

Alaska

California

The West has many different landforms. There are glaciers in Alaska and volcanoes on Hawai'i. Giant redwood forests grow in Oregon. Deserts cover parts of Arizona, California, Nevada, and Utah. The Rocky Mountains run through Alaska, Washington, Idaho, Montana, Wyoming, Utah, Colorado, and New Mexico.

About 65 million people live in the West. American Indians, Asians, Hispanics, and people of British and German backgrounds make up the largest cultural groups. Nearly four million people live in Los Angeles, California. It is the region's largest city.

Web Crawler

Trace important events in the history of the West at **www.pbs.org/ weta/thewest/events**.

Discover the West's natural wonders by clicking on the states at **www.nps.gov**.

Alaska
Malaspina Glacier

The Malaspina Glacier in southeastern Alaska is made up of many smaller glaciers. It is 40 miles wide and 28 miles high. Malaspina Glacier is so large that the entire glacier can only be seen from space. It became a National Natural Landmark in October 1969.

Arizona
Barringer Meteor Crater

In the desert of northern Arizona, there is a massive hole in the ground that stretches about 4,000 feet across and 550 feet deep. In 1902, Daniel Barringer suggested that a meteor created the crater. He then purchased the land from the U.S. government. Since then, scientists have learned that the hole was created nearly 50,000 years ago by a 150-foot-wide meteor. The site became a National Natural Landmark in 1967.

California
San Andreas Fault

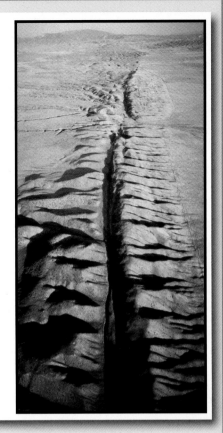

Earth's crust is made up of plates that shift very slowly. Two of these plates meet in western California. The boundary between them is known as the San Andreas **Fault**. It is a line of broken and crushed rock that branches off into smaller faults. Here, Earth's crust slides in opposite directions, causing earthquakes. The San Andreas Fault became a National Natural Landmark in 1965.

Colorado
Garden of the Gods

Located in Colorado Springs, Garden of the Gods is a public park made up of unusual rock formations. There are many hiking trails throughout the park, which also is a popular site for rock climbers. Garden of the Gods became a National Natural Landmark in October 1971.

Hawai'i
Mauna Kea

The Big Island of Hawai'i is made up of five volcanoes. *Mauna Kea*, which means "White Mountain," is one of these volcanoes. However, it is no longer an active volcano. Mauna Kea is often snow-capped in winter and is the tallest peak in the state of Hawai'i. Though about 18,000 feet of Mauna Kea is under water, it rises another 13,796 feet above sea level. If measured from its base on the bottom of the ocean to its peak, Mauna Kea is taller than any other mountain on Earth. It became a National Natural Landmark in 1972.

Idaho
Big Southern Butte

Big Southern Butte is found near the center of Idaho's Eastern Snake River Plain. It is made up of two volcanic domes joined together. There are

three of these domes in the Eastern Snake River Plain area. Big Southern Butte is the largest and the youngest of the three. It became a National Natural Landmark in January 1976.

Montana
Red Rock Lakes National Wildlife Refuge

Red Rock Lakes National Wildlife **Refuge** is found in southwestern Montana. Its lakes and cold-water marshlands attract many types of birds, such as peregrine falcons and bald eagles. The refuge is best known for its efforts to save the trumpeter swan from **extinction**. Animals, such as black bears, moose, fox, elk, beavers, and badgers also live there. Red Rock Lakes National Wildlife Refuge became a National Natural Landmark in May 1976.

Nevada
Valley of Fire

In April 1968, Nevada declared Valley of Fire a National Natural Landmark. The area is named for the brilliant color of the rocks when the Sun shines directly on them. The sandstone and sand dunes that make up the Valley of Fire are at least 150 million years old. Ancient Pueblo peoples visited the area about 2,000 years ago. Their **petroglyphs** have been found on the rock walls within the area.

New Mexico
Ship Rock

The Navajo call Ship Rock *Tsè Bit'a'i*, meaning "rock with wings." They believe a bird brought their ancestors from northern lands to New Mexico. Ship Rock represents this bird. Standing 1,400 feet above the plains, Ship Rock became a National Natural Landmark in May 1975.

Oregon
Newberry Crater

Newberry Crater is found at the top of Newberry Volcano in the Cascade Mountain Range. Many eruptions over about 500,000 years caused part of the volcano to collapse and form a crater. In 1976, it became a National Natural Landmark.

Utah
Joshua Tree Natural Area

Joshua trees are a type of yucca plant that grows like a tree. They are found in dry parts of North America. The Joshua Tree Natural Area in southwestern Utah is the only Joshua tree forest in the state. It became a National Natural Landmark in October 1966.

Washington
Point of Arches

Point of Arches is made up of rock formations called sea stacks. It is found off the coast of Shi Shi Beach in Olympic National Park. The rocky shoreline is home to many different **ecosystems**. In June 1971, Point of Arches became a National Natural Landmark.

Wyoming
Como Bluff

Como Bluff is a long ridge of land between Medicine Bow and Rock River. It is well known around the world for the **fossils** of about 250 types of dinosaurs that have been found there. Today, a gift shop and small museum are found at Como Bluff. It was named a National Natural Landmark in 1973.

The Midwest

The Midwest is in the center of the United States. It lies between the Rocky Mountains in the west and the Appalachian Mountains in the northeast. The Ohio River separates the Midwest from the South. Canada lies to the north. There are 12 states in the Midwest. They are Illinois, Indiana, Iowa, Kansas, Michigan, Minnesota, Missouri, Nebraska, North Dakota, Ohio, South Dakota, and Wisconsin.

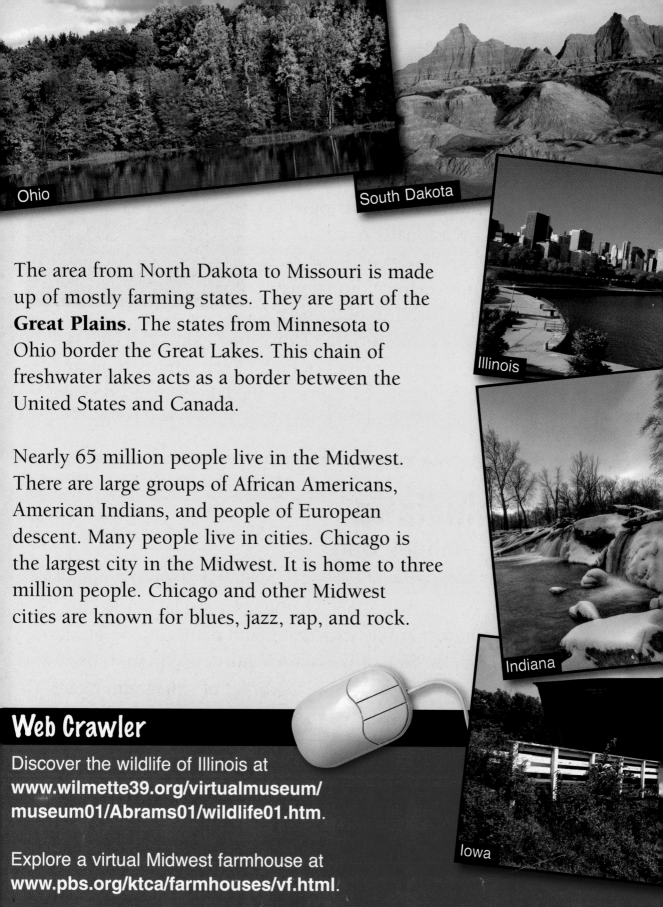

Ohio

South Dakota

Illinois

Indiana

Iowa

The area from North Dakota to Missouri is made up of mostly farming states. They are part of the **Great Plains**. The states from Minnesota to Ohio border the Great Lakes. This chain of freshwater lakes acts as a border between the United States and Canada.

Nearly 65 million people live in the Midwest. There are large groups of African Americans, American Indians, and people of European descent. Many people live in cities. Chicago is the largest city in the Midwest. It is home to three million people. Chicago and other Midwest cities are known for blues, jazz, rap, and rock.

Web Crawler

Discover the wildlife of Illinois at www.wilmette39.org/virtualmuseum/ museum01/Abrams01/wildlife01.htm.

Explore a virtual Midwest farmhouse at www.pbs.org/ktca/farmhouses/vf.html.

Illinois

Horseshoe Lake Nature Preserve

Before flood banks were built, the Mississippi River would occasionally overflow in spring. When this happened, the river would sometimes change directions and carve a new path. An older part of the river was cut off, forming Horseshoe Lake. The lake is known for hosting many types of birds. Each winter, thousands of Canada geese migrate, or move, to the lake. Horseshoe Lake became a National Natural Landmark in November 1972.

Indiana

Pinhook Bog

Pinhook Bog became a National Natural Landmark in October 1965. The bog is a glacial kettle, or a hole that fills with water and plants after a glacier melts. One of the main features of Pinhook Bog is

its carpet of sphagnum moss. Like a sponge, sphagnum moss can hold a great deal of water. In Pinhook Bog, the moss floats on the water and can be 3 to 6 feet thick in parts. It is the only true bog in the state of Indiana.

Iowa

Loess Hills

The Loess Hills stretch from Westfield, Iowa, to Mound City, Missouri. They are made up of loess, a wind-blown silt mixed with sand and clay, that was left behind by water, air, or ice during the last Ice Age. Shanxi, China, is the only other place in the world that has loess hills thicker than those in Iowa. Iowa's Loess Hills became a National Natural Landmark in May 1986.

Kansas

Rock City

Rock City is a collection of about 200 huge rocks on a section of farmland that is the size of two football fields. The rocks are lumps of sandstone that have been stuck together by **calcite**. No other place in the world has as many of these types of rocks of such a large size. Rock City became a National Natural Landmark in January 1976.

Michigan
Tobico Marsh

Tobico Marsh is one of the few remaining freshwater coastal wetlands in the Great Lakes. Found on Saginaw Bay in Lake Michigan, the marsh is about 1,652 acres. Open water, marshlands, and dense hardwood forests are three habitats found in the marsh. Many waterfowl use the area's marshlands. Tobico Marsh became a National Natural Landmark in January 1976.

Minnesota
Itasca Natural Area

The Itasca Natural Area became a National Natural Landmark in 1965. Lake Itasca, the headwaters of the Mississippi River, is found in this area. The virgin red pine, Minnesota's state tree, covers much of the land in this area.

Missouri
Big Oak Tree State Park

Amid the farmlands near East Prairie there are more than 1,029 acres of preserved land. This vast stretch of treed area is Big Oak Tree State Park. Located within the park, there are giant trees, including five of the largest trees in the state and two of the largest in the nation. As well, there are more than 150 types of birds and a boardwalk for visitors to view the park. Big Oak Tree State Park became a National Natural Landmark in 1986.

Nebraska
Ashfall Fossil Beds

Perfectly preserved skeletons of animals that lived millions of years ago have been found at Ashfall Fossil Beds. The animals died after breathing in ash from a volcanic eruption, which preserved their bodies. Remains of rhinoceroses, three-toed horses, birds, camels, turtles, and a saber-toothed deer have been found at the Ashfall site. It became a National Natural Landmark in 2006.

North Dakota
Two-Top Mesa and Big Top Mesa

Two-Top Mesa and Big Top Mesa are large land formations that look like table tops. They have a flat top and very steep sides. Mesas form when parts of a rock are worn away by rain and wind. They mainly are found in very dry

environments. Two-Top and Big Top are 1 mile apart from each another. They became National Natural Landmarks in October 1965.

Ohio
Cedar Bog

Cedar Bog State Nature Preserve is a protected area measuring 427 acres. Cedar Bog is a **fen** that was left behind by melting glaciers about 12,000 to 18,000 years ago. The glacier also left behind places for many plants and animals that are only found in the Cedar Bog area. The endangered spotted turtle, Milbert's tortoiseshell butterfly, and the Massasauga rattlesnake are a few of the animals that call the bog home. Cedar Bog became a National Natural Landmark in April 1967.

South Dakota
Cathedral Spires and Limber Pine Natural Area

Cathedral Spires and Limber Pine Natural Area are part of the Needles. This is a series of granite pillars that have been **eroded** by wind and rain. Located in Custer State Park, the area became a National Natural Landmark in May 1976.

Wisconsin
Cave of the Mounds

Cave of the Mounds is a limestone cave that formed about one million years ago. It is named after two nearby hills called the Blue Mounds. Many different minerals have been formed in this cave, and it is sometimes called the "jewel box" of major U.S. caves. Cave of the Mounds became a National Natural Landmark in November 1987.

The South

The South is made up of 16 states. They are Alabama, Arkansas, Delaware, Florida, Georgia, Kentucky, Louisiana, Maryland, Mississippi, North Carolina, Oklahoma, South Carolina, Tennessee, Texas, Virginia, and West Virginia. The Atlantic Ocean borders the South from Delaware to the tip of Florida. A part of the Atlantic Ocean called the Gulf of Mexico stretches from Florida's west coast to Texas. Mexico lies to the south.

Natural Landmarks

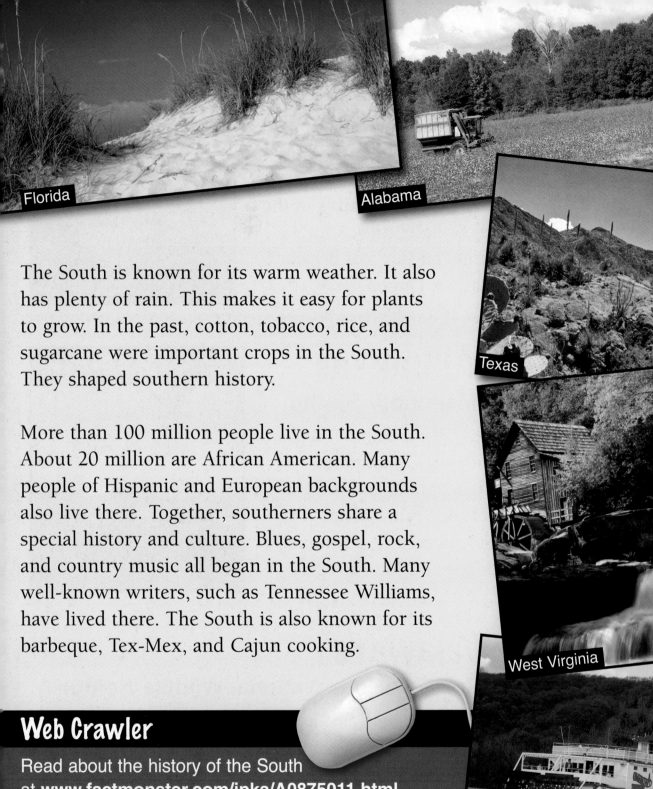

Florida

Alabama

Texas

West Virginia

Mississippi

The South is known for its warm weather. It also has plenty of rain. This makes it easy for plants to grow. In the past, cotton, tobacco, rice, and sugarcane were important crops in the South. They shaped southern history.

More than 100 million people live in the South. About 20 million are African American. Many people of Hispanic and European backgrounds also live there. Together, southerners share a special history and culture. Blues, gospel, rock, and country music all began in the South. Many well-known writers, such as Tennessee Williams, have lived there. The South is also known for its barbeque, Tex-Mex, and Cajun cooking.

Web Crawler

Read about the history of the South at **www.factmonster.com/ipka/A0875011.html**.

Explore the fun facts about the Southern states at **www.emints.org/ethemes/resources/S00000575.shtml**.

Alabama
Cathedral Caverns

Cathedral Caverns State Park is home to one of the largest **stalagmites** in the world. Called Goliath, it is about 45 feet high. Cathedral Caverns became a National Natural Landmark in 1972.

Arkansas
Mammoth Spring

One of Arkansas' largest springs, Mammoth Spring is a 10-acre pool and the headwaters of the Spring River. Mammoth Spring became a National Natural Landmark in June 1972.

Delaware
Bombay Hook National Wildlife Refuge

Delaware does not have any National Natural landmarks. However, Bombay Hook is an important migration spot for more than 250 species of birds. It connects a chain of refuges from Canada to the Gulf of Mexico.

Florida
Big Cypress Bend

Big Cypress Bend became a National Natural Landmark in 1966. Found on the border of the Everglades, it has nearly 215 acres of protected lands. Nine endangered species live here, including the West Indian manatee and the Florida sandhill crane.

Georgia
Okefenokee Swamp

Thought to be the largest swamp in the United States, Okefenokee Swamp became a National Natural Landmark in 1974. American Indians called the area *Okefenoka*, meaning "land of the trembling earth."

Kentucky
Big Bone Lick

Big Bone Lick became a National Natural Landmark in 2009. Ancient animals, such as mammoths, giant sloths, and mastodons, once lived on its land. Back then, the land was a swampy marsh. Today, it is made up of grasslands, trees, and shrubs.

Louisiana
Mississippi River

Though Louisiana does not have any National Natural Landmarks, the Mississippi River is important to its culture and economy. Running through 10 states, the river begins in Minnesota and ends in the Gulf of Mexico. It is the second-longest river in the United States.

Maryland
Sugar Loaf Mountain

Sugar Loaf Mountain became a National Natural Landmark in June 1969. It is a **monadnock** that rises 1,282 feet above Barnesville, the town at its base. It is of great geological interest and a popular recreational area.

Mississippi
Mississippi Petrified Forest

The Mississippi Petrified Forest became a National Natural Landmark in 1965. Here, 35-million-year-old maple and fir trees have become fossils. It is the only forest of its kind in the eastern United States.

North Carolina
Pilot Mountain

Pilot Mountain rises 2,421 feet above sea level and is the focal point of Pilot Mountain State Park. Pilot Mountain got its name from the American Indian word

Jomeokee, which means "great guide" or "pilot." There are two pinnacles, or points, on the mountain, Little Pinnacle and Big Pinnacle. Pilot Mountain became a National Natural Landmark in May 1974.

Oklahoma
Salt Plains National Wildlife Refuge

In June 1983, Salt Plains National Wildlife Refuge became a National Natural Landmark. The refuge was created for migrating birds. More than 300 species use it throughout the year, including Canada geese, snowy plovers, bald eagles, and peregrine falcons. As well, Salt Plains National Wildlife Refuge is an important natural habitat for whooping cranes.

South Carolina
Congaree River Swamp

Located almost directly in the center of South Carolina is the Congaree Swamp. This swamp is a wildlife

sanctuary that contains the largest cypress-gum tree swamp and hardwood forest in the state. The Congaree Swamp became a National Natural Landmark in May 1974.

Tennessee
Lost Sea (Craighead Caverns)

The Lost Sea became a National Natural Landmark in 1973. It is the largest underground lake in the United States and the second-largest in the world. The Lost Sea is part of a cave system called Craighead Caverns. The caverns were used as a meeting place by the Cherokee. Scientists found the footprints and fossils of a **Pleistocene** jaguar in the caves in 1939.

Texas
Dinosaur Valley

Dinosaur Valley contains some of the best preserved dinosaur tracks in the world. Found in the Paluxy riverbed, scientists have used the tracks to find out how and where the dinosaurs walked. The site became a National Natural Landmark in October 1968.

Virginia
Virginia Coast Reserve

The Virginia Coast Reserve is a National Natural Refuge for many waterfowl and birds. It became a National Natural Landmark in March 1979. The Virginia Coast Reserve is a safe environment for the birds that use the area for migration or breeding.

West Virginia
Cathedral Park

Located on 133 acres of land, Cathedral Park is the largest forest of untouched timber in the state. Its massive trees are protected from being cut down. Cathedral Park became a National Natural Landmark in 1965.

The Northeast

The Northeast is the smallest region in the United States. It is east of the Great Lakes and south of Canada. The Atlantic Ocean borders the Northeast coast. There are nine states in the Northeast. They are Connecticut, Maine, Massachusetts, New Hampshire, New Jersey, New York, Pennsylvania, Rhode Island, and Vermont.

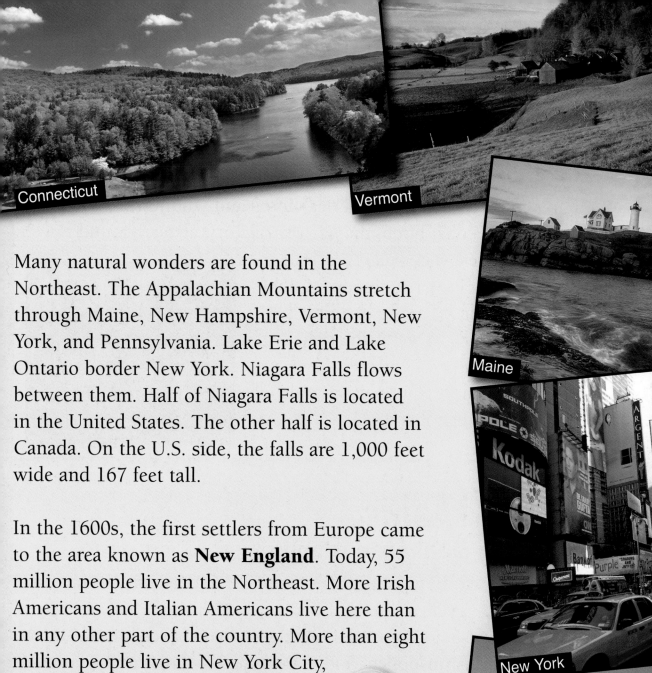

Connecticut

Vermont

Maine

New York

Pennsylvania

Many natural wonders are found in the Northeast. The Appalachian Mountains stretch through Maine, New Hampshire, Vermont, New York, and Pennsylvania. Lake Erie and Lake Ontario border New York. Niagara Falls flows between them. Half of Niagara Falls is located in the United States. The other half is located in Canada. On the U.S. side, the falls are 1,000 feet wide and 167 feet tall.

In the 1600s, the first settlers from Europe came to the area known as **New England**. Today, 55 million people live in the Northeast. More Irish Americans and Italian Americans live here than in any other part of the country. More than eight million people live in New York City, the largest city in the country.

Web Crawler

Learn more about New England at **www.discovernewengland.org**.

See spectacular views of Niagara Falls at **www.niagarafallsstatepark.com/Destination_ PhotoGallery.aspx**.

Connecticut

Bartholomew's Cobble

Bartholomew's Cobble is made up of rocky knolls, or cobbles, that rise above the Housatonic River. It is home to a great variety of North America's ferns and wildflowers. Trees, such as pine, oak, birch, maple, and hickory, also are found there. The freshwater marshes and beaver ponds in Bartholomew's Cobble are home to many types of animals and other plants. Due to the rich variety of life there, Bartholomew's Cobble became a National Natural Landmark in October 1971.

Maine

Monhegan Island

Monhegan Island is a small, rocky island off the southern coast of Maine. The northern half of the island is covered in a dense, red spruce forest. Much of the island is unspoiled, and many types of birds can be found there. Monhegan Island became a National Natural Landmark in April 1966.

Massachusetts
Muskeget Island

Muskeget Island is only 14 feet above sea level. Sand dunes make up the northern shore of the island. The southern shore is mainly composed of marshes. This island is the only known home of the Muskeget vole. It is also the

southernmost point in the world where nesting grey seals are found. Muskeget Island became a National Natural Landmark in April 1980.

New Hampshire
Mount Monadnock

Mount Monadnock became a National Natural Landmark in May 1987. The mountain stands 3,165 feet high and has little soil surrounding the peak due to fires that took place in the late 1800s. Before the fires, the mountain was covered in a forest of red spruce. Slowly, this tree is growing back up the mountainside.

New Jersey
Great Falls of Paterson-Garrett Mountain

Great Falls of Paterson-Garrett Mountain became a National Natural Landmark in 1967. Together, the falls and the mountain show how volcanic lava

flow helped shape the eastern North American landscape during the Mesozoic era about 245 to 65 million years ago.

New York
Long Beach, Orient State Park

Long Beach in Orient State Park is one of the best examples of a sand-gravel spit. The 2.5-mile long beach illustrates the change from a salt marsh to a red cedar forest. A type of bird called the roseate tern is common to the area. Long Beach became a National Natural Landmark in 1980.

Pennsylvania
Presque Isle

Presque Isle is a **peninsula** that was formed by sand carried on the currents of Lake Erie. The area is constantly being reshaped by winds and waves. Many migratory birds are found here. It became a National Natural Landmark in 1967.

Rhode Island
Ell Pond

Ell Pond is a kettle-hole lake that is surrounded by a swamp of red maple forest and Atlantic white cypress trees. It became a National Natural Landmark in 1974.

Vermont
Camel's Hump

Camel's Hump is the third-highest mountain in Vermont. At one time, the entire mountain was covered with fragile plants. However, warm temperatures have made it impossible for them to survive on most of the mountain. Camel's Hump became a National Natural Landmark in 1968.

A National Natural Landmark

National emblems are symbols that are used for the entire country. The American flag, known as the star-spangled banner, is one such symbol. Another is the bald eagle, which is the national bird. The oak tree is the national tree. There are many National Natural Landmarks across the United States. An example is Walrus Islands in Alaska.

Walrus Islands are a group of small, rocky islands found in northeastern Bristol Bay, Alaska. They are the only place in the United States where bull, or male, walruses gather in large numbers.

About 4,000 bull walruses gather at Walrus Islands in the summer. The walruses haul themselves onto the beach after they spend a number of days feeding.

Walrus Islands became a National Natural Landmark in April 1968. It also is protected as a state game sanctuary.

More About Walruses

Walruses are marine mammals that live in the shallow parts of the ocean in Arctic regions. There are two main types of walrus, the Pacific and the Atlantic. They have large tusks, sensitive whiskers, and enormous bodies that weigh between 1,800 and 3,700 pounds. Walruses eat mollusks, shrimp, crabs, tube worms, and sea cucumbers.

Guide to Natural Landmarks

A NATIONAL NATURAL LANDMARK
Walrus Islands, Alaska

ALABAMA
Cathedral Caverns

ALASKA
Malaspina Glacier

ARIZONA
Barringer Meteor Crater

ARKANSAS
Mammoth Spring

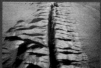

CALIFORNIA
San Andreas Fault

COLORADO
Garden of the Gods

CONNECTICUT
Bartholomew's Cobble

DELAWARE
Bombay Hook National Wildlife Refuge

FLORIDA
Big Cypress Bend

GEORGIA
Okefenokee Swamp

HAWAI'I
Mauna Kea

IDAHO
Big Southern Butte

ILLINOIS
Horseshoe Lake Nature Preserve

INDIANA
Pinhook Bog

IOWA
Loess Hills

KANSAS
Rock City

KENTUCKY
Big Bone Lick

LOUISIANA
Mississippi River

MAINE
Monhegan Island

MARYLAND
Sugar Loaf Mountain

MASSACHUSETTS
Muskeget Island

MICHIGAN
Tobico Marsh

MINNESOTA
Itasca Natural Area

MISSISSIPPI
Mississippi Petrified Forest

MISSOURI
Big Oak Tree State Park

MONTANA
Red Rock Lakes National Wildlife Refuge

NEBRASKA
Ashfall Fossil Beds

NEVADA
Valley of Fire

NEW HAMPSHIRE
Mount Monadnock

NEW JERSEY
Great Falls of Paterson-Garrett Mountain

NEW MEXICO
Ship Rock

NEW YORK
Long Beach, Orient State Park

NORTH CAROLINA
Pilot Mountain

NORTH DAKOTA
Two-Top Mesa and Big Top Mesa

OHIO
Cedar Bog

OKLAHOMA
Salt Plains National Wildlife Refuge

OREGON
Newberry Crater

PENNSYLVANIA
Presque Isle

RHODE ISLAND
Ell Pond

SOUTH CAROLINA
Congaree River Swamp

SOUTH DAKOTA
Cathedral Spires and Limber Pine Natural Area

TENNESSEE
Lost Sea (Craigshead Caverns)

TEXAS
Dinosaur Valley

UTAH
Joshua Tree Natural Area

VERMONT
Camel's Hump

VIRGINIA
Virginia Coast Reserve

WASHINGTON
Point of Arches

WEST VIRGINIA
Cathedral Park

WISCONSIN
Cave of the Mounds

WYOMING
Como Bluff

Parts of Natural Landmarks

The National Park Service surveys sites to see if they meet the requirements of the National Natural Landmarks designation. When studying these places, the service checks if these sites fit into specific categories. Many sites that have been designated as National Natural Landmarks do not fit perfectly into one category.

TERRESTRIAL ENVIRONMENTS

Terrestrial, or land-based, environments might be home to endangered species, a unique combination of species, or an indigenous plant or animal that needs to be preserved and protected. These places are made by natural processes, likely taking thousands of years to develop.

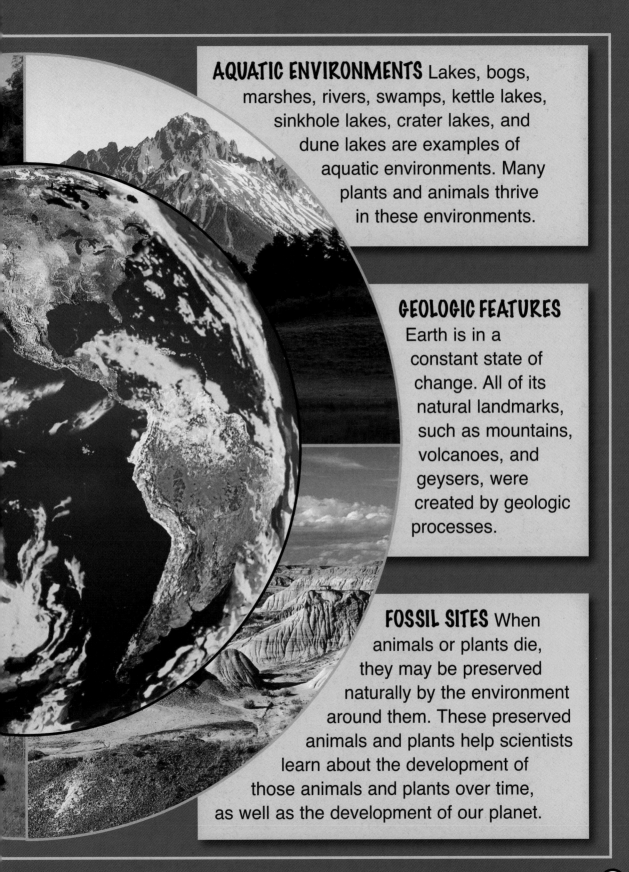

AQUATIC ENVIRONMENTS Lakes, bogs, marshes, rivers, swamps, kettle lakes, sinkhole lakes, crater lakes, and dune lakes are examples of aquatic environments. Many plants and animals thrive in these environments.

GEOLOGIC FEATURES Earth is in a constant state of change. All of its natural landmarks, such as mountains, volcanoes, and geysers, were created by geologic processes.

FOSSIL SITES When animals or plants die, they may be preserved naturally by the environment around them. These preserved animals and plants help scientists learn about the development of those animals and plants over time, as well as the development of our planet.

Test Your Knowledge

1 Which National Natural Landmark has one of the largest stalagmites in the world?

2 Where is Mount Monadnock?

3 What does *Mauna Kea* mean?

4 What is the southernmost point in the world where nesting grey seals are found?

5 True or false? Ship Rock is a 19th-century clipper ship.

6 What is the third-highest mountain in Vermont?

7 In what state are the headwaters of the Mississippi River located?

8 What state has a refuge for the nearly extinct trumpeter swan?
   a. Nevada
   b. Alabama
   c. Montana
   d. Connecticut

9 What National Natural Landmark was created by a meteorite?

13 What is Cathedral State Park known for?

10 Where are some of the best preserved dinosaur tracks in the world?

14 What is Presque Isle?

11 The second largest underground lake in the world is located in:
a. Arkansas
b. Tennessee
c. California
d. North Dakota

15 True or false. Loess is a fertile soil for farmer's crops.

12 How old are the trees in the Mississippi Petrified Forest?

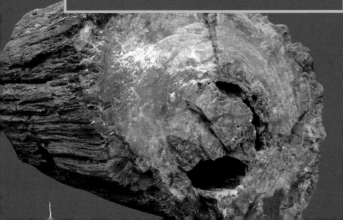

Answers:
1. Cathedral Caverns, Alabama
2. New Hampshire
3. White Mountain
4. Muskeget Island
5. False
6. Camel's Hump
7. Minnesota
8. c. Montana
9. Barringer Meteor Crater in Arizona
10. Dinosaur Valley in Texas
11. b. Tennessee
12. 35 million years
13. being the largest forest of untouched timber in West Virginia
14. peninsula
15. True

Create Your Own Natural Landmark

How do scientists know that a glacier has been in a certain area? How can they tell which direction a glacier was moving? Try this experiment to find out.

Materials

a plastic or paper cup | tape
gravel | a paper plate
water | a smooth piece of wood
plastic wrap

Directions

1. Fill the paper cup with gravel.
2. Cover the gravel with about 1 inch of water.
3. Tape plastic wrap tightly over the top of the cup.
4. Turn over the cup, and place it on the paper plate.
5. Place the plate with the cup inside a freezer overnight.
6. Remove in the morning, and peel off the plastic wrap.
7. Scrape the icy gravel over a smooth piece of wood. This is similar to a glacier moving over the land.
8. Observe the patterns the gravel makes on the wood. How would this compare to patterns made on the land by real glaciers?

Further Research

Many books and websites provide information on natural landmarks. To learn more about natural landmarks, borrow books from the library, or surf the Internet.

Books

Most libraries have computers that connect to a database for researching information. If you input a key word, you will be provided with a list of books in the library that contain information on that key word. Non-fiction books are arranged numerically, using their call number. Fiction books are organized alphabetically by the author's last name.

Websites

The United States National Park Service website is full of information on all the National Natural Landmarks in the country.
www.nature.nps.gov/nnl

Earthquakes are major natural forces that create all kinds of landforms. Find more information at this site.
http://earthquake.usgs.gov/learning/kids

Glossary

biological: relating to living things

calcite: a white or colorless mineral

ecosystems: communities of living things and their environments

eroded: worn away by water, glaciers, wind, waves, and other elements

extinction: no longer existing any place on Earth

fault: a break in a body of rock

fen: low land that is covered partly or entirely by water

fossils: rocklike remains of plants and animals

geological: the study of Earth's history, structure, and rocks

Great Plains: a vast grassland region covering 10 U.S. states and four Canadian provinces.

monadnock: an isolated hill or rock

New England: an area in the northeastern United States including Connecticut, Maine, Massachusetts, New Hampshire, Rhode Island, and Vermont

peninsula: an area of land almost surrounded with water

petroglyphs: carvings or line drawings on rocks, made by ancient peoples

Pleistocene: a period beginning about 2 million years ago and ending 10,000 years ago

refuge: a place of shelter or protection

stalagmites: cone-shaped mineral deposits

Index